DEED

KUHL HOUSE POETS

edited by MARK LEVINE

and BEN DOYLE

DEED

Rod Smith

UNIVERSITY OF IOWA PRESS *Iowa City*

University of Iowa Press, Iowa City 52242

Copyright © 2007 by Rod Smith

www.uiowapress.org

Printed in the United States of America

Design by Richard Hendel

The University of Iowa Press is a member of Green Press Initiative
and is committed to preserving natural resources.

Printed on acid-free paper

Library of Congress Cataloging-in-Publication Data

Smith, Rod, 1962–

Deed / by Rod Smith.

p. cm.—(Kuhl House poets)

Poems.

ISBN-13: 978-1-58729-619-2 (paper)

ISBN-10: 1-58729-619-5 (paper)

I. Title.

PS3569.M537962D44 2007

811'.6—dc22   2007008811

07 08 09 10 11 P 5 4 3 2 1

[CONTENTS]

[THE GOOD HOUSE]

for Amy Wright

the egret says

the house, it is something to eat or sunlight, the egret

thinks, the house, it wills, is a subcanvas I can scribble, the egret moves

or is awake, loving the familiar solution of loving, this explains

      the egret to the egret in the house

to the house & sunlight, we become intelligible because the egret

      says elliptical,

in beckettland or geography, in small mammals & planets

no egret never not says elliptical, no elliptical egret mechanism

      well under a love, today, or today,

      does not increase elliptical, covered stand of egret then,

the sunflower freezing in the egret's reason

      is spilling nutria, is an idea

&

affiliative, monthly, in egret pajamas, lolling, to

merge with the sunflower, frozen in not freezing, but flashing.

egret lights, they stretch, & revere, they say
i have a thing,
instruct in the new circumstance, elliptical,
tangible, to their sweet ego, in open-heart &
patagonia, go beyond shy in time they gain
& haunt, let's say
the word of the egret is
thumb, let's say thumb
as an egret prelude then, in order to correctly translate sappho, &
        think the cluster-egret, its
didn't get through water, its
safely egret waning
or education of sweet ego thumb then
in time or in
the night did dawn & the whales did spout
as a kind of paperclip on our idiots
all graphic kindness
& all graphic kindness
& to you, my egret soul, all is ooh, & all is
pronounced like a bell, & all is between me proposed,
pursuing one's own all, so to ring, & so to ring

THE GOOD HOUSE

The good houses the parts, calls to
them, & wakens—

    in being, the house we will, its precepts
    lumber the stilling male—
    opulence isn't allowed, so to
    form is to erase what's not
    gradual & new — a specific
    love to focus the elements

    when we lock the door
    things float around awhile,
    climax, & rest

    in the new sense

———————

The good part of the house
is where something leaves
alone the light that it lattice
the red, souring, hoarse
needs made by no
other — safety depends in
them—
    so knowing strength
    so knowing weakness

this is where we will, & home

———————

The good house feels bad about
the territory
                    — the house seems
to be a verb though it dislikes
the term 'housing' — the house
seems to be a bad dog & a
live wire — the house is bored
until people come over — the house
is anxious to please guests —
it is stupid & so thinks cordon
means love — it is wise & so
chooses —

    the honesty of the house helps
    the people to know — they can
    relax & recall other houses
    they have known, they become
    simple & listen to each other
    & to some birds, the birds right now

————

The good wasn't built into
the house but earned, once a beggar
lived there, & once a small one—

the police came & went

there were parties

————

The good was an upkeep

It was a perilous upkeep

There was kindling

———————

This house was that house
to many— & to many there was no
house there because they hadn't
noticed— there was one who
noticed & was wanted, was loved

this gave the house hope
this gave the house no hope
this gave the house hope

it alternated. sometimes house, sometimes home

———————

& sometimes the kitty licks the bicycle on the porch

———————

there's a barrel in the basement
that belongs to a country singer
named Nel—

there's an old wonderbread wrapper
behind the kitchen cabinet nobody
knows the story on—

there's a stack of bad news in
a box by the back door—

there's a wreath in a box behind the thing
& a bauble on the windowbox above some stuff—

————

tears never house us, maybe they
cleanse, maybe they don't, the word
intend doesn't seem to fit

sentiment

————

anything can be made out of a house.

though many of them are blue.

there's a kind of recovery in it then.

too much innocence, or minutes
left out, those.

a time, or economic worry, a
weird abreaction.

seeps
in the house are loans one cannot trust.

a trusted house, the work of
the house, a dirigible.

seeps in the house should not be imagined.

————————

the worst is not good, it's alone & not nourish

————————

time is a housed reputable beginner

thirty more are needed

tripping, the house kneads the flower,
spells me, parts the bowl, stuns
& is soft, stuns
& is real

————————

the good house is given advice:

In times of danger ceremonious forms are dropped. What
matters most is sincerity.

———————

There are 8 houses in the heart,
there should be 9.

———————

That it is a house.
That it never moves.
That it loses concentration.
That it questions
& foregoes — does not feel
good — does not
hail —-

    half of it, for love

     harbinging

   & voracious
        saplings
     of prayer—
       praying to
saplings, lots

   of lazy, happy, lenient

   bested cognizance, the felled

   soft letters of coming.

———————

the good house — it is heavy,
the good house — it exercises
hope in the inhuman, is transformed
by it—

    becomes blatant in its strength
    & is destroyed, the good
    house must be rebuilt
    carefully. The good house
    is in conflict.

———————

ordinary houses complete

the smart bombs and are

buoyant — victorious,

brainwaves of shunt commotion,
bestial then or not house

—the load— the
makeup assignment reads long

into the long night, dreams

of lassoes, garbage, things

it thinks it cannot change.

———————

Each reasonable house
& each waking motion
are votive, based on
the wiley resurgence
of awaiting worlds—

—————

House & holographic, pastoral
battenings brace
the heart's chosen will
which being one thing,
becomes modest,
plies the decent roads
w/ nests & rope, lone
& casual, available
breezeway of won seeming—
this house, it is
safe & loving, protected
from what is false
unfailing — then no wince
can raise or pillar night
thence town—
      house await
      & house be grown—
      house of house heart
      of house, a lake
      be side, it is sown.

—————

Any sung house requires
calligraphy, camp, &
curtains — all too cute yes
yet one tires of burnt
toys, dry fetishes, dead
humor, & clocks. To hold
that which one loves
in the right way, with
trust & lust, w/out
a certain kind of winter—
to love the one one loves
& be loved
in a good house
for a long time

———————

Ordinary lung, ordinary
life— late
belonging willed— the yet
wild— the yet
known
or commonplace still—
Fall to this
that it come again
of need to be the given close

for the good house
is at an angle, for the good
house of heat, ordinant
like glue, gone again
like glue

———————

day one in an apple— angstworthy
whiles widening the awake,
dreaming— it is a because
isn't turning— so,
        with those clothes,
            so,
        with those soaps—

mostly no wilt in the choose

the clothes on the floor are calm

the clothes on the floor arouse

whaddya say, let's not go vote today

————————

Leave the leaves, let them
work— this will
would rather
underrate that— when it's
like that

                thanatos turpentine
            or teacher's bepetment
        a spell
            toked in the coatroom,

    sunning.

————————

The house in Crimea, is it good?
we don't know
but it goes on— it is important.

Several, unreasonable.

House spite comes when there's
no plants. Coughs & dragons,
the said empire is tight,
woe to causation— woe
to the swart angles

————

In a quiet house
In a house which is very quiet
Where the brackish tandem brooks
the loons

It is cold

It is cruel, somewhat erotic,
wavey like a top what was
a spool—

     the inner standing
     is ten to the Nth

     'power' — we think
we house, actually we are housed

& the equal quiet shakes in us

————

House of one or house of two,
house
      to be drawn up, house
      to be new— the day
      or this, thanked, returns
      the unburnt house, returns
      the milling world

————

Though the house is willed it is also shiny — though it
spares others, some it doesn't, though it has a child,
it is clear, stolid, imperious— though it laughs at the
waking needy, it compels grace, walks awake the named,
any of them, any & others, clear it has, clear it laughs,
house though some, house & rescue, also shiny, in the
sounds made, in the sounds created, in the sounds &
in their laughing, it is a house to be reckoned with, built
in the mania of inaction, a still, unbuilt shining thing where
the knowing crosses into every, where you would, & the
sounds are made tame, & the sounds til, & the house
sounds, & because, & I would do the house a favor,
& fill this sounding, & would is shiny in the sounds, built,
unbuilt, a laugh or child of them, the sounds, the grace,
the poetry of the house, its seeming, but it has never
seen itself sound, yet its knowing can, because there is
no false in it, again it houses as it had & has house being,
green eggs or ham, & puts Peloponnesian there, shiny,
holding the deranged oracle by the ear, making its
wishes, housing the one it loves, with a sound

————

The flourish in the house might
tower above the other concerns
but eventually it tires out &
has a makeup day.

Perhaps this is a rescue fantasy

The mention is the house in this case

Its loams & wills warp the partake

Yet there is a well from which to drink

The water is not good unless it is clear

––––––––

This reverie noodles the lovely house
like the pleasure of not reading
a badly written headline.
The technology of transcendence
is a speaking, infinite, rescindence.
It does not matter if we trust
the house. Because I am the one
speaking right now I can say
we. Therefore I think, to the
degree that you can, you should
trust me.

––––––––

The ground of the house is what
the useful things grow from.

The ground of the house has always been there
as far as we're concerned.

———————

Nefarious
                underlearnings
tile the worn sturdy,

                our tanks are thankless

                a treatise grown
                into a clattering
                wayside strump—

then the house creaks, riotous,
& the year's angles bid
for moss because it's hard
to breathe, because an encapsulated
mania droops, & a pall of
recognition billows in the surfeit
waist

———————

the rhythmic heartening house
& gentle return, & gentle
to be believed must be wed
to the ratio of need — wisdom
for the half-heartened
implies a certain humming
in the halls, of the circulating
pump, where the branch supply
pipe, unadorned, rises
vertically through the fortunate
parquet past the goose-neck
to radiate its rising warmth—

the bleeder valve
& column placate the striation's
un-nixed imaginary—

     the good house is curled
& blunt
   inside
     an instrument shelter
whose construction-
     play is paced
w/ nonexistence, the pale
cornice of what this is
reads back the
wanderer's return — a danger
    which is distance come back, the trees
hang high in the heart
where hope is built
& nurtured

———————

If the house is just poetry
we're in trouble.

————

blade-shaped, bending
in, creative ——
          a need
          a part, it in peril

          housedrone & damage,
          piled in the road

          like a person

————

     houseperson, co-
     opted strength of this

stayed apart, person it's gone

————

house against us, house
trounce,

      the way to underbecome it
— no, it is
possible, this
life or not, this
trust, it must

    stave love

    stirred

    then amidst

     & what equal
     & what quiet

      —if it is
a story, make
of it
      no menace

    to what actually
happens.

————

It would be best
if no one pretended.

The will
whether human, nascent, or
lathered, sings
to the banana & bicycle,
breaks us, a nut
like a brick, goes
backwards, pales in the
modus operandi—
we cloak
the individual
wheel & come apart
like cookies.

_____

The good house
        summers on Long Island, reads
Debord, & rests
like a scythe, well-oiled, fervent—
vehicles permeate
        & are colossal— think
the knots, think
the mobius core

_____

Cheery
& it's moving, copious

trilateral intoning
shmooze, which is to say-away
what a good house
moans,
knot embedded,
suffering & bold

_____

The good house gave away a certain
sincerity. It got bought up. But
the ravages of equality rack it—
not unforced, not unburied, the
good house or murmur

    displays its living air
    & punted, rides
    the miracles, foamy—

If the house were to be unlived,
which it is, what ideal decadence
could undermint the
contoured, stylistic, yearning
of the satisfied whiles
of crux— it serves the vivid
involuntary american, born
at the weighstation, raised
on the right wing, bent apart
by breaking
hearts, yet unblamed, the
bills reading the skies as they
die, & our world
is done.

―――――

The good good house, the stake

in samsara, loaded on

Sierra Nevada, screaming

at the game.

————

Go inside, good house,
& do not clone, do not
reconcile, rather groan—
for what is good hurts too.

    the sudden crunch chords
    no longer surprise the
    heathen clan, & the mellow
    tunes tho nice, settle
    on the mind like make-up

if you're thrown by saturnalia
if you're taking that nap
if completely fucked up

call what parts
shed the wizening
lobotomy of lurid beams—

that it not will us
that it renegotiate, carve
into, & fell the wacking
unworn stasis

that it strangely spell this
or time, & remake the road
that it will not us
to the unfolding implode

this & stopped.

this & begin.

——————

the dive-bombing of the house
by raconteurs & pigeons
is a more than not-so
copious loping fetid
ordination padded,
stirred, laced, running
them on the Moe, tacet
& confused — blue gaunt
lackies orphaning the pills.

————

"Most men are so boring."

————

In history, hangovers
like sounds, have a basic
changeless core, which
is based on natural
principles of studious
renewal, self-denial, &
attraction. Once one,
shallow, pulls the funny
string to ring the ding a ling
so that the arrows, in flight, might
acquire their difficult
expedience,
        the rosey half-eaten
durations pale,

necklacelike,
        before the deathlike
carry-ons, which stay the no
                        upward,

a bouquet of dispersion. its burial.
in a basement or a growth.

————

The beauty of the house—
it is quite a spectacle,
such are its lies, implied
taut sexual learnings
& severed territorialities—
addictions, reductions.
incoordinations, blue-blank
astral tempts done-up for
gone-off, diming the ire
of penance— a beam or
gang lanced — thin again
& blue where you, & a tortoise,
find those that would be new.

————

House, o
you there— pinebare
of want & stuffed—
those other takebacks
away then, house the
unwanted evil, grow it in love
& go w/ swim
to the carnival of come undone—
it's boney & cerebral, bent
on your american butt—

O house the waves
kill the weak, wash awake
the unspent hurt
of happenstance enemies,
grill us
our breast & cloaked
periodic collapse—
it's unlikeable, the beast
they have to offer, simply
the beast we have.

————

O house, o o o, &
house of verb & house of
go, the house
now dormant dons its
better love & stun,
de-housed, the fold,
up to it, flailing.

a house
· your house
a house
filled w/ meaningless shit.

—————

No one in the intellectual
house lops off lust have ya noticed?
Way over in the way apart
off-touch like off-color
looms in the web on offer,
lists of swarms of wannabees
broke-backed in coeval sniffles
pop-n-fresh or cohort the morse
angle of retreaded lov-anguish
in peril or pert hope, placated
by the overfed nothing whilst
creating their foamy fate
w/ mist in crates on dates
        —— draw a line in the
bag. step over. &
steep in the understand.

—————

House it has walls
House it & house of
That fat house

On tour

Terrorizing the thinly educated
worst, moist, bumbles

horny

collapsible—

      the home
      of severing gnosis
      implied in the microdot,
      the depthcharge
      on the screen licking
      its photosynthetic wilts
      —how the tissues are
      strengthened— how the pump
      beats— how the soft outer
      self houses the soft
      inner guts.

———

The house is form, not a stagecoach
or common
spot but a sung threefold maw
to define to live & one
          is the form of the medusa's fingerpaint
          to spread the abundant waste
          & two
          is the form of the safire
          to spread the abundant waste
          & three is the form of the causeway
          — a reft, banal
          window to fill the abysmal
          flaming — nothing
          cries in the form,

          learning us good.

          ———————

Then the house
is popping — happy house
on a hill in a valley by
a brook. There it is, & will
be, til it was.

          ———————

House or not, it's a hummer ey?
Rotten house—- I mean how could you?
Home to the hotcakes & the slosh—
a lolling barnacle of embarrassed
clocks, the hothouse & the heaps
of no, smothered by the nuckle—
stiff as a cock—

———————

That it, once good,
gathers in & grates, or
koalifies like a spurn—
the raucous perilizing
unlumbered flops like a
seabird, & o I am afraid—
let those which search
the knees comfort then the whorls,
a ply popped, loading, &
the filched
ports plummet in us our
turned loam, the nascent
ordinance craning in the
flu, or you there,
locked in before,
lax & radiant, less pre-
natal & less apparel, the more
one you, the less than two.

———————

"Excuse me officer, I thought
you were a shape-shifting rat."

———————

The impossible ones, their
hats & glowing, tensile
ammendations— tearing
the wonder, its increments—
better to be lefthanded, hauty,
burrowing, then askance

like a clarity

———————

The natural laws, & the longing
of the house— its hero variants
stalk the vestibules
like cormorants, seeking
new skills & other pests, pepper
to put on the belonging, a stereoscope
of the casual surfaces, pecked
through, the learning underneath.

———————

Peace can be made w/ the house—
haven then, or half haven half
pander— the ruins
& the beautifying
link the thought *that*—
an unenforced local lean-to,
lax in the peril, but spacious.

———————

only so much danger
will fit in the house, only so much
style— when raining
or when
unimpaired, the house looks
out & out, lunging— apparent
listless tilling, in Pembroke,
in the nascent stopover, the
breathing house, those who
mend the fence, the list
of attributes, the pile of bills
for those attributes, the
basement of regard, a place
to single out & carry on—
housed one
amidst else, sometimes tired,
not undone, the soft tasks
of inner truth,
      the relative weights
of relatives & relativity, the
absolute, its circular motion,
& the making, & the making.

———————

or house tone. lone
thing
    tending— the secrets
in the spring, an ordinary
faultlike effervescing, still,
        lazy in the
        filmy wristwatch
        of shambles—-

      aspirant
    tarnished
    dome— dry as authorial grace,

the lame undoing of the spent
pulling. paring
the reasonable treelines, a washing
of the made, its name

———————

the egrets have come back to
the good hut — the egrets
hasten our retreat, peal
apart the tempting, stolid,
spare, inept grace
w/ egret stuffing, w/
narrativity, shamanistic
foodlike thingys
in storage, out-patience, & plumage
the egrets lift or can lift
large televisions which they drop,
the egrets are wise
& do not fail to understand.

———————

Housenight, the way a house
happily unfolds, because it
isn't buried, because
the disencumbered, pre
or entailing, hothouse
never severs but cups, houselike,
the dreamstate,
the housed part

the closed inside then

a kind of waiting always

[THE SPIDER POEMS]

Nothing believes Korea.

Nothing turns into it, & leaves your salt there.

For it to fade, for it to ask casually, how's your Rothko?
how's your thrift store

painting? how's that? Nothing believes Korea.

& believing it believes also
that to be afraid is accursed, caseladen, peripatetic, inchworthy &
glown. That's what it believes.

Nothing much worse than that.

Nothing much worse than for it to fade that way.

In the second part Korea disappears, becomes

quasi-angular, like a filter, like a soup, like a spider

suddenly in your face. Suddenly, this is the poem
in which the sudden spider is suddenly in your face.

Like a spider.

These are spiders. They are happy spiders.
They fill the bugles of the nut-brained beaming
throughscape most happy to collate.

Other spiders live in the soft languish of the original underpants.

Come, live with the spiders, come, join them,
in the long hibernation dream of the original underpants, Mr. Jones.

Some of the spiders are not called anything because they are happy.

This is my new style. How do you like it?

It has caused me great personal anguish.

Franklin Covey & the spiders are coming down from the Natl Capital
carrying torches & poems.

Nothing believes them.

These are seeds being planted which are growing spiders.

Growing spiders need milk to make strong bones. I have no milk & so

they are mad. I have no milk & so

they are very, very, mad.

Mad spiders all over the place. I believe them when they say

"we are mad."

I go out immediately & buy lots & lots of milk.

I give it to them & then I run.

Once you've raised the expectations of the spiders you've imagined

You can then write things like "forms of forms are the reasoned mock alone in the ice factory eating whistling homeless quesadilla" &

"be well, runt" & "what is love but a layered lookalike leaning on your bauble"

Feel free to write these things like those things. & remember, an ant the size of a rat may well be attacked by a hawk.

PART 2 (MORE SPIDERS)

After closing, & in closing, nobody's fault, & nobody's business
begin again to break, & having broken, to placate
the charms afforded by the first natural warm feels
& a cute abrasion, kind of
curly, & hicked, hurled through the roof-window
which allows the letters more-than-minute shack factory
to fill up & infold a facticity lunging upwardly languiding &
blue says & blue gentle rocks hurt
most of the often people 7 times, got that?

Having wantings of spiderlike facticity
& wantings also, awake in laundry, & laundry also,
awake in wanders which are very clean.

Having those you should have them & so do.

"I miss the urth."

Goodbye.

Spiders are very interesting folks. Most of them are thieves
who do not want anything. If you are a thief who does not
want anything this does not mean you are a spider. It shows,
rather, your lack of creativity.

Nothing left, 'cept chapstick.

Spiders have needs of webbing.

If you are a network you are improperly loaded.

Dust on the old spiders & dust on the
resumé, dust then & there,

dusty spiders all over the place. &

Small tacks. Unbrandished but highly & speckled, speaked
spider
the whilst lent dumb of
spider

it it left of spider & also
stilt

it is a lazy spider to be placed on the fellow with the rat for a head

In my life o this life. yes, this one. o, it.

In it, there have been spiders. o, spiders.

etc.

PART 3 (MORE URTH-VOICES & SPIDERS & STUFF)

The spiders have or can have all sorts of spilling.

Some of the spiders become violent at the drop of a hat.

Some of the spiders are getting ready to have been smushed

by that hat. Each spider has its destiny & pride. Each spider

is a clump of spider longings & thrills. The perceptions

of the spiders & the areas they retread. The perceptions

of the spiders & the long walks around the dam along

the cordon. One is stupid.

Clearly the detritus of spider-process spears the tiny yet flatulent advisors. Let none say that anything said is unsaid, excepting anything said by everything. We are the witch mission & the drought. Everything is saying anything watching the flavorless respite. What do you say we say? The spider-process spears the respite. What do you say we say?

I hate the man who investigates hidden matters.

I hate the spiders.

Scared & infinite, the wipped, stunned spurts pop the placated junk-spider, stoving. Watch yon spider yawn. Watch the furling wills can the rasps of spider will. Each foretold tin is a lint spider rioting. Each foretold tin injures the basket. Stand back in the spider. They would not have known injustice if it were not for these things.

The spiders can or can't stand there at Austerlitz. The spiders can or
can't leave alone Springsteen's America. Fill your spider pockets,
if you have them, with
spider envy & lust. Saying why
is like saying spider. Fill your why with walks with spiders,
they will heave through you, & each,
like lairs which are love awake in spider death & rebirth,

in spiders of melting, your brain, in spiders
of wanting, your heart, in spiders
of seeming, no beat, in spiders
of nothing, no wheat,

turn Austerlitz over, turn awake
the rabid spider
heart.

[THE GIVEN]

Barnes & Chernobyl

It's got everything you need

It's an artist

It don't look back

Poem

sacred

        dumb guys

standing in the fake world

        flipping out

I, eating eggs & April, looking back over holding her name
here in the soft night of textual survival where the Goose
Gossage nameplate alliance has no service economy it can
call its own. Thin, possible sonnet awhirl in the roast caked
cognition making red breast storied beets out of nothing
for my love that the robes they sport become heavy
— the good one is resolute, has combines & rides you
prizing the difficult weapon sickness & saying "not is injured"
to the perfect shunning rope-weary high in its acting &
in its acting & in you there being them to the rakes
which are rakes, and granaries, very empty

The Given

clarity, & calm assonant
asphyxiation
It is a shunned soft
out-cut
eclipse decrease

There's no way out
by my death or consciousness

lying on the frivolous ground
wearing frivolous gowns
babbling about wands and pucks
inside the musculature hush

Moist Feelings: A Love Poem

Every now & then
I feel you ignore me

Knee-deep in lust

I turn around &
look at you
& you're not there
because you're not you

It feels like something
Wet and ugly
Has taken my place

It smells like strawberry surprise

Identity Is the Cause of Warts

i have a toad. its name is buber. buber the toad. buber raises rabbits. the rabbits live in a big can named big can. or rabbit can. mostly they complain. buber bangs the lid for them to calm down. it doesn't work. at the last annual convening of the international monetary fund buber spoke to a packed house about toadstuff. he talked it up good & the bankers banged their lids. sometimes buber & me smoke pot. other times usually while banging buber has a twitch of sympathy but always for himself & he calls the phone & it says anything so he bangs on it too & i feel sorry for it & hang around with all these other things in the room wondering about this banging toad in my life. buber gets a bygosh bygolly expression which on a toad looks like all their other expressions but that toad'll sing "Little girl I don't work in no candy kitchen / Na & I don't sell no chewin' gum." do any of you folks have toads. can you help me through my toad difficulties. sometimes i lie asleep all night. i just can't take it anywhere anymore. sometimes i think i should get a frog instead but my friend jigs casey has a frog & he built a nuclear weapon with it & i'd really appreciate it if you wouldn't call me anymore.

Ted's Head

So there's this episode of Mary Tyler Moore where Ted's trying to get a raise & after finagling and shenaniganizing he puts one over on Lou & gets his contract changed to non-exclusive sos he can do commercials which is not cool w/ Lou & the gang because Ted's just a brainless gimp & it hurts the image of the news to have the anchorman selling tomato slicers & dogfood so Lou gets despondent because the contract can't be rescinded but then he gets mad & calls Ted into his office & says, "You're going to stop doing commercials, Ted" & Ted says "why would I do that Lou?" & Lou says "Because if you don't I'll punch your face out" & Ted says "I'll have you arrested" & Lou says "It'll be too late, your face will be broken, you're not gonna get too many commercials with a broken face now are you Ted?" & Ted buckles under to force & everybody's happy, except Ted but he's so dumb nobody cares & everybody loves it that Lou's not despondent anymore he's back to his brustling chubby loud loveable whiskey-drinking football-loving ways. Now imagine if Ted were Lou, if Ted were the boss. You know how incredibly fucking brainless Ted is, but let's imagine he understands & is willing to use force. That's the situation we're now in as Americans.

Specifically the Luminous

crossing the frozen
popular manners in
cotton night's
ancient dun plat
a monochromatic chintz
seeped (however large)
in upon us burning & adjusted.

Still, the exclusions
Rent saying,
Reciprocal, Fluid,
To the power consumed
To the rising & to the
Stunt ocean. Inept.
Encircling these
little songs.

The Strength

In the renting & in
something lengthy
a loosening, a lack's lattice
round— this beam abbreviate opposite-sized carnal loam—

it is its sever

triad is not so low as to shove a gone stop

& then the solve curses
& thin the corpse ago

— dawn runs it, dawn, that is.

the rising's recourse.

alone.

Floorboard

mist is similar to certainty. alas
& discover, a calming
earlier
half-lit
committed quitter bottoms out on the mad grub.

& wince to speak
sepia.

& oppression.

looking for daddy in the burn again I
was born & read up on
consideration.

listen. not on your life—
but in.

human in the brew.
pitching like a bottle.
minutes.

It's a light in a dry dispatch, done away from, the theories in the junk, dusted & tagged, rapping awake the message from the ferns— "if it is light, let that be a crying repetition, formerly introspect faults in shaded catchword willy-nilly singularities coaxing the raining loss from the measured undergone" — fragile, no? fumbled like a pullover seems sometime alight with laxity, not too slumberous, small next to the unfolding displexity, to start the smart-learnt unlit lightly, a time neither safe nor circular, bound toward its irreversible tainting, each one's own history, unfailing— that makes it a meal, or a maim, or a mass of lanterned wastrel science under-become by their just insouciance, a vibe de-blip brunt forcing burial into time, time into pits, pits of their unmade life— ants on Venus, varying their routine, place an incongruent list of programmatic social upheaval beside the pillar on the balustrade to opine peanut-encapsulated furrows, an opine-like situation-device fault-imploded, backlit by the social coping, caustic in the ant revolution, yet sated, Venus at an unswart angle revolving and clothed, a clothed planet never paralyzed, its peaks dents in the groan of gastric internecine cosmology, a guide for the thoroughly moisturized tourists, they tell the story & then they leave to tell the legend, & then they leave, having exhausted their collective nothing, widely, some of them have been bit— yet it is not back at all, that fanning out of sanity found in fatal thinking, solids more timely than saints, saints?— sacrifice —the luckiest of them drown pseudo-cyclical specificities, dampen their motes of sorrow-spun shunting in a meek sound environment of bell-lacking bench-strewn upper partials, thirteen-colored & secret, the lands in the not-Venus of light awry, autotoxematic machinations of cosmic causistry causing small bluntings to the ant-imagined axis deer doing donuts in the fantasmic materialization, they are thus driven into madness, mad deers all over the place, mad in the razor, mad in the guise— what ideology already was, deer society has now become— the gods when they go, which they don't, are dialectical informatics arranged radically on the hunter's scopes, a blight informs their brisk cognition, a blight of crying repetition, these god-workers on strike, getting fat on counterfeit proletarian justification, becoming lyric, almost individual, where the taps played in the cistern stoke the post-Ayler continuum awake, rattles & cameras, baked bads on sale after educationary exercises masking the more-fake-than-thou excess of the canopied canapés, truculent & sad, raiding, forlorn, in a ruckus, borrowing pills, affirming, lush, clackety-clack, click-sent bedevilings of this awkward minute, returning to the regal listening, someone's little essay about something shattered like a desire, your desire, shattered like someone's little something about an essay— these are them, those deer offered bananas on their flight to Bermuda, but they don't want them, being full, yes, of canapé, and crying repetition has become their bailiwick, tho they cannot find institutional support for these interests, much less an avant dissonance to soothe their not so savage fawnings— if it fails — the natural cycle of sleeping — if it fails — the wicked mice of plus signs apparent to the mashed open retreads pulp-lisped parental softenings cut apart by the paste & parrots, we crux, we are shared, like lettuce, like merits, like the brains in the skulls beside the airs on the grounds above the goings, that, there, those, then, thick awake refascinated leapings in a letter, or something vague, something almost not there, a something garish contracted from contact with fragments, & so we are in the dark alone, like everything else, & maybe there is some light. Maybe we can see it.

the love that is truly a refuge for all living beings

Thermal Deformation of The Active Element Of A Periodic Mode
like the previous
moment of a ball of foam, but with regard
to the sounds that were, so to speak,
thrown away
through the process of making other pieces,
like the sprout from a rotten
seed, water music, impurity-induced
self-trapping of holes
and minority-ion percolation
like the erection of a eunuch,
like antennas,
and some were
like interruptions
of photoelectric
cells, living became something quite long that could be cut
up, stabilization of
stimulated extended-life emission like
thoughts of avarice, immorality,
wickedness, and hostility
in a bodhisattva who has attained tolerance,
photochemical, or
any other form of punctuation
the effect of the four
refractive indices
like the perception of
color in one blind
from birth like
the fun of games for one who wishes to die like
Blackbody radiation when I whispered it and cadences
became things
free of conceptualization an empirical

luminescence discharge the
syllable passion spectra into the electric
fanning halide laser
a vast anomalous
reactive tangent
activity's
constructual
alms—
properties of properties dent
in welding this
weak collision, aeons
of foci— tunable, coherent,
immeasurable

of the abstract scene in the book jacket photo
doesn't have a setting so much as a latent impenetrability
not unlike the lenient, bitter, bracketed latticework
of emotion I'm culled to reincode for no reason
lost, or lone & lost, or leftover & lost, or lacking loss
based in a brick sickness of stilted words
the scene leans in, fortunate, unmasked,
taking its saturate incongruence to the hilt.

Witness the solemnity
as an excuse for however central
such simple shapes sound in a show
of coloured lights under the eves & notice
how subtle the supple learn
the other's graffitoed violence.

or a shapeless mass?
or a loaf of tawdry
shinola? or a list of fictions like days like stars burning
like ideologically judgmental harmonies out of their trance
a wake— patience
plus
thematically lactate spirits in neutral space
yearn into the dreary cone it passed pale to taunt that step
that blatant sleep
that singular individual instance of one it.

weird.

yet monochromatic war was no longer satire so much as some
technophobe totem experimenting over the balcony
in the gas he goes to call
& is stirred by —
but managed somehow to boast

anyway, something about a drinking problem
or a missing arm or an alien culture
but I stopped it there feeling the terms alien & culture extremely personal
& felt the danger, the literal urge
in fact to actually say something about
micromanaged alienation &
the experience of audience participation as portrayed in the
soft porn novels of my own two-teared society.

Nevertheless, this urge passed & was lost, was gone, was

jettisoned, was judiciously disearned, & left out—
the lathes of the intervenient chaos locked in on the smiling
clenched dust revealed to me in that light thus spoke or the
sound of a footstep which unfolds which for it to be what it
is for itself I give up & look up

This is why the sick child falters in a field of abstraction.
This is why chaos can be so disheartening to those who would
control their lives. This is why the stalactites must be left in
place for the next clumsy oaf. You are not here! Heads or
tails with ink in it. Open &/or closed in the amused
swerving, almost always unable to find the underlined passage.

XCVII ("she knows who she is")

for what we are, swart passion
"amount" (the liaison debt)
    six & 1/2 to one, or the Having will acquire
SILVER as the need's I
    and just as false
    "and just as false"
as chide triangulated mist sinks me or me
                (rivulet of competent

purse & grave, a gravity
relent in peace to stand bled
& strain. each out to false.
to turbulence. to time before
that codes grief cycle
    gist in the tones & riled re-wave
        says, and so is, and so the lowly
can be saved,
        but from

           purpose
      & turbulent, the taste
        is troubled,
& an accordance
abutts transcendence
      & crushes us, internal
for the thought doomed strong
        does not tense in it
          "we" are a crime
or foundations, effectively mist
felled before   current events
a crisp descent, not innocent
        the complacent bit's history
              a cretinous
      aggregate, a young explorer, but the net

torque canned against the likes o

                              that gaze

worn scrupulum's caste of ash
      le livre
the torn internal
in the right honorable reticence
             take it back
             that
hitting head moment
June 9th, '68
           Cape Thing
             off the coast of Superficiality
snored in a cone — a brave deed
      you can drive around
but to imagine that, a somehow made not nascent
      rent by shade
"maybe partying will help"—
      but within love's coy tract
shave that soldered salve (ouch)
        is formed or is our failure or is
      a tongued environment's impetuous debility
they keep us locked up layers of non-sent slapping
      love in the purified finite
a gasping torqued thought-finish
on the effective mist
      this ludicrous business
this sadly ossified empty
        final, injured, found waning
      an orchestrated probable praised by motion
it's circuit that again torn is thought they locked
      blazing in the blazing
say to it this form's shunt seed
say to it "closure"
as a clanged jack assays a coral cloud-document breath of

tazed intent
in the growth aglow
    the bombed fundamental
        re-bombed futz of gut-us consumpt
  & wayward   leaning on a star

[HOMAGE TO HOMAGE TO CREELEY]

Poem for Stingers

Nothing static is a syrup.

Nothing is out of nowhere except syrup.

Is syrup on a photograph trying to enter the picture?

Syrup.

Hurrah.

Hurrah.

Syrup is a stage name for Drano. Too much Drano would burn the little boy's finger in the dike. This is likened to a stinger.

This is a poem about a bug husk.

The little boy's finger, is it a stinger?

Does the little boy go bzzz bzzz?

Wrong Turnstile

The perpendiculate particulate
& its official placemat replacement
propel all the parts expelled
to a pre-date.

On this date, the not yet circles
an abbreviation. The circles are
now on the abbreviation. Maybe they
always were.

I don't know if this is about the weather.

Weather is something that's "outside."

I love you.

Circles in the hand can be stolen, but who can rob this weather of its own treasure? The last thread of love can be stripped away, but a naked circle covers all. Fools, like circles, in the Santa Fe morning light, cannot be encircled, because of the ever-vigilant ACLU. What would you have me hide under silk and the glittering of jewels?

Shadows Are Our Friend

To discover the rabbit/duck requires a certain amount of light.

A rabbit can duck, & does, in the presence of predatory birds,

into shadow. This does not help the rabbit if the bird is an owl.

Do owls ever feel happy? My guess is no.

This might be about a short-term relationship I had.

This might be about a short-term relationship I had

shortly after my son missed a curve at midnight

on a full moon. There is some reason to believe

he was trying to miss a deer.

The Life of a Dime

A dime does not think.

This makes it enigmatic.

The dime thinks "I do not think"

"This makes me enigmatic"

A bad poet might then write

"A penny for your thoughts"

This would not be worth a dime

The erotic idea of a or the erotic dime is a dense erotic eroticism of erotic longing says the bread & circus thief to the analyst, erotically.

Old dimes are removed from circulation & treasured. Or melted down.

Does this resemble consciousness? I still love you.

pour le CGT

We work too hard.

We're too tired

To fall in love.

Therefore we must

Overthrow the government.

[ACKNOWLEDGMENTS]

Selections from "The Good House" have appeared in the following journals and online publications: *Aufgabe, Beltway* (online), the *Germ,* and *Raddle Moon.* The entire poem appeared a chapbook edited by Katherine Lederer with silkscreen cover by David Larsen (Spectacular Books, 2001). "The Spider Poems" was published with work by Lisa Jarnot and Bill Luoma in the chapbook *New Mannerist Tricycle* (Beautiful Swimmer, 2000); it also appears in the DC Poetry Anthology at dcpoetry.com. "Specifically the Luminous" was selected by Ann Lauterbach to receive the Greg Grummer Award and was published in *Phoebe.* "XCVII ('she knows who she is')" and "the love that is truly a refuge for all living beings" appeared in *Protective Immediacy* (Roof, 1999). Other poems in this collection, in the original or in translation, were published in *Anomaly, Articulate, Boxkite* (Australia), *Cartografitti* (online), *English Matters* (online), *Explosive, Gare du Nord* (France), the *Germ, i.e. readings broadsides, Idoei* (Sweden), *Lingo, non* (online), *Poésie* (France), *Radical Society* (U.K.), *Shenandoah, Signature Series Number One, 26: A Journal of Poetry and Poetics,* and *Vinduet* (Norway).

"The Spider Poems," "Homage to Homage to Creeley," and "Identity Is the Cause of Warts" appear in French in the volume *Poèmes de l'araignée* (Bureau sur l'Atlantique, 2002). "Ted's Head" appeared in *Music or Honesty* (Roof, 2003) and in the anthologies *100 Days*, edited by Andrea Brady and Keston Sutherland (Barque Press, 2001) and *Enough*, edited by Rick London and Leslie Scalapino (O Books, 2002). Selections from "The Good House" appear in the anthology *19 Lines: A Drawing Center Writing Anthology*, edited by Lytle Shaw (Roof Books, 2007), and in the bilingual anthology *Walt Whitman Hom(m)age 2005/1985* edited by Éric Athenot and Olivier Brossard (Turtle Point Press, 2005).

Many of these poems appear on the CD *Fear the Sky* (Narrow House Recordings, 2005).

The author would also like to thank Anselm Berrigan, Leslie Bumstead, Jean Donnelly, Buck Downs, Heather Fuller, Peter Gizzi, Mel Nichols, Alexandra Smith, and Mark Wallace, for everything.

KUHL HOUSE POETS]

David Micah Greenberg *Planned Solstice*

John Isles *Ark*

Bin Ramke *Airs, Waters, Places*

Bin Ramke *Matter*

Michelle Robinson *The Life of a Hunter*

Robyn Schiff *Worth*

Rod Smith *Deed*

Cole Swensen *The Book of a Hundred Hands*

Cole Swensen *Such Rich Hour*

Tony Tost *Complex Sleep*

Emily Wilson *The Keep*